Hairless

Hairless

Breaking the Vicious Circle of Hair
Removal, Submission and Self-Hatred

Bel Olid

Translated from Catalan by Laura McGloughlin

polity

The translation of this work has been supported by the Institut Ramon Llull.

Polity Press
65 Bridge Street
Cambridge CB2 1UR, UK

Polity Press
101 Station Landing
Suite 300
Medford, MA 02155, USA

ISBN-13: 978-1-5095-5018-0
ISBN-13: 978-1-5095-5019-7 (paperback)

A catalogue record for this book is available from the British Library.

Library of Congress Control Number: 2021947547

Typeset in 12.5 on 15pt Adobe Garamond
by Cheshire Typesetting Ltd, Cuddington, Cheshire
Printed and bound in the UK by TJ Books Limited

For further information on Polity, visit our website: politybooks.com

For you, who might want to know
whether you want to.

And for all those women who have helped me
do what I want to.

Contents

I

History of an Obsession

I decided not to shave anymore.

The deciding part is important: from puberty until that day, I'd spent a large part of my life not shaving, but there was no conscious decision to challenge anything behind it. Like so many women, I felt obliged to do so if my legs, armpits or groin were going to be on show in public, and I didn't feel obliged to if nothing was going to be on show. After showering, I would play with the hair on my legs (always prickly from shaving them so often) and I'd think, 'One of these days I have to shave', and leave it until the hot weather came.

As a teenager, I would stare fascinated at the impeccable and seemingly smooth legs of friends

3

and wonder how they did it. My hair was rebellious, abundant, black. Waxing wouldn't pull it all out, and if I brushed my hand over the tender skin, still hot from the wax, I'd still be stubbly and not at all sensual. Within a few days, it would be the same as ever. Every time, the beautician promised that with this new technique I wouldn't have to come back for a month, and every time it was a lie. When it was already undeniable that, yes, once again my legs were hairy, I'd don my trousers and avoid the beach until I ended up going back there: the torture of hot wax; red, sensitive skin; hair peeping out, threatening.

Hair removal creams did leave my skin smooth, but it was an illusion that lasted barely a few hours. The hair grew even faster than with waxing and was more stubborn, as if enraged by the aggression. The other option, shaving my legs, was a long, tedious task. I would often cut myself and the itchy nicks would be with me until the itch of newly sprouting hair turned up.

My absolute failure when it came to keeping my hair in line was more than a practical failure condemning me to trousers and beach-less days: it was a clear failure of my femininity. I already felt like an impostor in the role of a girl: I performed the best I could for fear of becoming lost and finding myself even more alone than I already was, but I knew that the long locks and dresses were a lie that I was painfully sustaining. The fact that hair persisted in climbing up my legs, sprouting uncontrollably and ever more plentiful, and my inability to tame its stubborn bushiness were unequivocal signs that, no, I wasn't a real woman.

My mother said it was my fault. I wasn't disciplined enough with waxing; I gave in too early to the razor. Actually, waxing was expensive; and my means as an adolescent, precarious. She had fine, light hair, and very little of it, and she only shaved once a year. Maybe if I had inherited that attribute from her, I wouldn't have seen the need for questioning hair removal, seeking to free myself from it. The easier it is for us to conform to the canon, the less violent what it imposes on us seems. But conforming has never been my strong suit.

It took me a long time to realize that the ads for shaving products, in which a hairless woman shaves to remain hairless, were a farce, and what was happening to me happened to many other women. In fact, I discovered this when I was 17 or 18 and I began going to bed with women more liberated than me, who invited me to caress them without worrying whether they looked 'presentable' or not, who offered me their open cunts without even considering what I would say about their bikini line. I was upset by such a lack of concern; I was a little irritated that they didn't play the game; I loved knowing they existed. I was profoundly shocked by the possibility of bodies that feel and vibrate and live beyond the norm, and I desired the strength to be one of them too. But while it was an important revelation, I didn't stop trying to appear 'normal'. Just if I was wearing a swimsuit or shorts. Just if I was wearing a dress. Just if I was undressing in front of someone for the first time. And so on, for many years, until the age of almost 40. Then, one day, I decided not to shave anymore.

Outwardly, practically nothing changed. The people with whom I shared a bed and intimacy were used to the bushiness of my groin, as intense and extensive and fragrant as desire itself. But I knew I'd decided not to shave, and this hair wasn't circumstantial. It wasn't an accident that had to be corrected as soon as possible, nor was it squatting on my skin. I'd labelled it a legitimate

6

resident of my body, and I planned to allow it to accompany me in sickness and in health, to the swimming pool and to the beach, until death (ideally, not mine) us do part.

The first day I left home in shorts with hair (lots of very long hair) on my legs, I felt absolutely vulnerable, yet euphoric. I didn't know what would happen, but I was breaking a very rigid norm. A norm which I had invested time, money, sweat and tears in to uphold. I felt proud of my decision and, at the same time, ridiculous for the undeniable slightness of the gesture. Thousands of women every day fighting for noble causes – extremely noble, extremely important – and yet here I was, proud of showing a bit of hair.

In the fluorescent light of the metro, my legs seemed even uglier than under the brilliant sun that June morning. I ran my hand over them, as if I wanted to smooth the hair. The woman sitting opposite stared at my legs, hypnotized. She pulled a face of surprise, or shame, when she noticed me looking at her, as if I'd caught her doing something bad. I pulled my legs back under the seat, hiding them as much as I could.

I'd left home thinking that, in that moment, finally, I was escaping gender norms and definitively stating my freedom to be who I was. But, rather than feeling euphoric and happy, I felt ugly and ashamed. The most important path, that of truly accepting myself as I am – not as a draft of the optimal version of myself, not in inverted commas, not accidentally because tomorrow I'll shave – was just getting started. And the hair on my legs was only the tip of the iceberg.

2

From Happiness to Shame

I don't know if the saying 'Where there's hair, there's happiness' is referring to genitalia as a particularly hairy place and potential source of great joy, but I like to think so. Even so, in the barely thirty years that have passed since I began to have pubic hair, the quantity of hair it is socially acceptable to have there has drastically reduced in general – and even more so for women in particular.

Women's depilatory habits have intensified in our society to the point that currently the only acceptable places for a woman to have hair are on her head, her eyebrows and eyelashes. It's not only permitted, but obligatory, to have it in these areas. All kinds of cosmetics and prostheses are sold – from pencils to darken brows to false eyelashes – to achieve the desired effect of localized luxuriance. Meanwhile, the industry of removing hair everywhere else on the body relentlessly advances. And not only that: the fashion industry and magazines express very clear implicit and explicit messaging. Hair is no longer a synonym of joy.

At the beginning of the twentieth century, the idea that beautiful women had to have smooth, hairless skin had already taken root. The difference from the present was the quantity of skin on show: practically none. Hands and face, and that was it. Even though we know that, 3,000 years before our time, shaving implements were already in existence and that in Egypt, for example, it was common for women to shave their heads and pubic areas, judging by the earliest 'racy' photographs this custom wasn't prevalent in the West at the beginning of the twentieth century. The Catholic Church played an important role in this change in habits throughout the centuries: during the Middle Ages, it spread the idea that removing hair from intimate areas was sinful, and thereby eradicated a long-established custom that had been, in fact, as widespread among women as among men (it was a matter of class, not gender: the hairless body was associated with a higher class, rather than a specific gender).

Centuries later, with the progressive loss of the Church's power, the higher hemlines rose and the shorter sleeves became, the greater the obligation to shave legs and armpits grew. So, while in Western society in 1905 you could grow up without ever in your life seeing any naked woman who wasn't yourself (or someone in your immediate family) – and therefore having no real means of comparing, or even contemplating, whether you were very hairy or not – in the sixth decade of the twentieth century audiovisual culture was firmly established and people were exposed daily to images of clean-shaven women wearing very little clothing. Comparing yourself with women seen in the media wasn't only possible – it had become inevitable. And it was very clear that the desirable armpits and legs were those that didn't have hair.

The stronghold of intimacy was still left to us, and everything that didn't stick out of a bikini was allowed to exist. The majority of pornographic films from the seventies and eighties would be labelled today as 'hairy pussies': that is, as an unusual fetish, and not normal or generally desirable. The strip of groin that must be maintained free of hair has expanded more and more in recent years, ending up conquering the whole pubic area.

As women's bodies have been increasingly uncovered in cinema and advertising, we've been able to compare ourselves to them – or, rather, we've been forced to compare ourselves to them. The lack of diversity and the fact that the only possible and desirable bodies continue to be those that don't have hair establish hair removal as an unavoidable tax on womanhood. The first time you shave is a rite of passage: you are recognizing that you are leaving childhood behind, and accepting that you have come to an age at which you can be considered an object of desire. And that age is becoming lower every day. The American waxing company Wax Candy claims that 10 per cent of its customers are younger than 13 years old. Some of the girls asking to remove hair from their legs are 8 or 9, and the reason is usually that they are being mocked at school.

The reaction of many families to girls being bullied is to eliminate their body hair, rather than to eliminate abusive behaviour at school or in wider society. The reasoning is clear: it's easier for the girl to remove her hair than to fight against the social machinery that pushes her to do so. But, behind it, there is an even darker reason: deep down, we agree that this hair shouldn't be there. How many child actresses of any age have we seen on television series or children's channels who have hair on their legs? Zero. Even though pre-pubescent girls are less likely than teenage girls or women to have much hair on their legs, it is not exceptional either, and even less so here in my Mediterranean home country.

The pressure girls are under not to have body hair goes hand in hand with the ever more intense sexualization they suffer. In 2014, controversy was unleashed when a swimwear brand intro- duced bikinis for girls of 9 with not only a bikini top, but a padded one, so when it was put on the wearer appeared to have breasts – 9-year-old girls with fake breasts to please whom? From where does this need arise? Who finds promoting these aesthetic standards desirable?

In public bathing areas, there are ever younger wearers of two-piece bikinis, which thirty years ago simply didn't exist. If you were a girl, you wore a swimsuit or bikini bottoms and that was that, at least until your breasts emerged. Marking the bodies of girls by covering non-existent breasts is a way of making them adopt the role of possible object of desire way before they might become desiring subjects, when still lacking the tools to cope with this implicit sexual gaze. The effect is even more toxic if, on top of covering non-existent breasts, we add fake ones as well.

Despite a campaign opposing the item at the time, and the brand being forced to apologize and to stop selling it, the uproar didn't last long, and today it's easy to find. Training bras are increasingly widespread, and many girls who don't yet have breasts wear them. Before puberty, *they are being trained* for what awaits them. Beyond the (questionable) necessity of wearing a bra when they have breasts, social convention dictates wearing one as an affirmation of a femininity linked to an increasingly precocious sexual availability.

But this movement is even more perverse: at the same time that we sexualize girls by lowering the age at which bras and hair removal are required, we infantilize adult women by requiring them to remove one of the unequivocal signs that they are no longer pre-pubescent: pubic hair. Having a completely bare cunt has been added to the list of requirements for being a desirable woman, a list which can be summarized like this: you must appear to be 20 if you're 40, 15 if you're 20, and you must never – whatever age you are – appear to be older than 30.

As well as the obligation to eliminate pubic hair, an aesthetic pressure is being exerted on women that was unheard of until recently: having a symmetrical vulva, with small inner labia, light pink in colour. That is, a young girl's labia. Many plastic surgery clinics offer labioplasties and, even though they explain that it can have advantages as important as 'being able to wear tighter clothing', on their own websites they confess that the majority of women who undergo this procedure do so for purely aesthetic reasons.

Removing all body hair from women and demanding little-girl vulvas contributes to the erasure of the acceptance that puberty marks an inviolable social cut-off point which must be respected by sexually active adults. It standardizes heterosexual men's objects of desire into a single group in which there are no age distinctions, in which girls of all ages, and women, have to obey the same rules. We're simultaneously selling padded bras to little girls of 9, and underwear with animal and cartoon prints to adult women. We are obsessed with not appearing to be adults, with erasing any sign of the passage of time (which should make us stronger, with better judgement and more tools to deal with sexist aggression), while contributing to the pressure on our daughters to make their bodies conform so as to satisfy the most toxic male gaze.

Paediatricians and psychologists are worried about the increasing number of girls who ask to shave to avoid bullying at school, and many articles, reports and interviews with specialists have been published on the subject in the media. Reading them, I was surprised by how few voices were critical of the social pressure around hair removal aimed at young girls. The majority of paediatricians consulted assert that, apart from laser hair removal – which isn't effective until past puberty and isn't worth doing beforehand – methods of depilation have no contraindications for girls' physical health. What they don't say is that they don't offer any positive health benefits, either. The psychologists, for their part, comment on the benefits that hair removal can have for girls who suffer violence from others (from schoolmates of the same age, but also from adults) who think they have more hair than they 'should' have. Instead of helping to launch an attack on the root cause of this violence (and recommending that we send the aggressors to a psychologist, for example), they recommend that we get rid of the girls' body hair.

But the long-term effects on the self-esteem of future women are clear: we are teaching girls to give way to the autocracy of society's control of their bodies, to reject their bodies as they are and modify them (even through painful procedures) in order to conform to an increasingly inflexible norm and submit to the tyranny of external 'desirability'. Because, if indeed, among the 'body police', there are boys and girls, women and men, this police always argues in favour of the male gaze and appoints the heterosexual man as a judge of what is desirable: 'no one will want you with that hair' (assuming that 'no one' equates to 'no real man').

There is no space for celebrating the bodies we have as they are, and the lesson we impart is extremely hard: if you want to suffer less violence, if you want others to like you, adapt to what is expected of you. At the same time, those who commit violent acts also learn that their intolerance has a reward: at the end of the day, it's simply a matter of keeping up the scorn and insults until women succumb and conform.

Claiming that hair removal is a personal decision, which we make freely with no interference from anyone else, can give us the impression of a certain sense of freedom, but we are deluding ourselves. It would be a personal decision with no further significance only if the consequences of removing hair and not removing hair were equivalent. When shaving has a social reward (how pretty you are) and not shaving attracts censure (how disgusting), the decision stops being innocent and becomes political.

If we want to end the sexualization of girls and the infantilization of women, if we want future generations to grow up truly more free, at some point we have to limit where we shave and at what age we begin to shave. Right now, we are ripping joy away from adult bodies while sowing shame in those of young girls.

3

Is a Hairy Femininity Possible?

It's strange that a characteristic feature of adult women – that is, the appearance of hair on the pubis and underarms (and often, though not always, on many other areas of the body) – is considered a masculine trait that must be eliminated completely if you want to appear undeniably 'feminine'. As we've seen, to look like a 'real' woman, you must actually look like a little girl. The pressure to make the bodies of girls and women the same is about a need to return women, who have clearly advanced in terms of rights and social recognition, to the archetype of the under-age girl controlled by men. The demands for women in a position of power to have an unmistakably 'feminine' gender expression are even greater than for other women; it's as though they have to compensate with their hairstyle, make-up and, obviously, impeccable hair removal for having invaded a space reserved for men. The first things for which female politicians are reproached, way before their political acts, is that they are ugly, they don't dress well, they don't know how to style their hair. This isn't merely a banal rehashing of gender stereotypes – it's also a constant reminder that the first thing they have to worry about is the eyes of others on their bodies. Through this alien gaze, men act as judges of what is desirable, and women as guardians of 'femininity': who is allowed to be considered 'a real woman', according to whether they follow the rules or not. The call to perform a seamless traditional femininity is an attempt to control and taint the power they've managed to achieve.

Lately, we've seen a few actresses, singers and models with hairy armpits or unshaven legs on show. The degree of acceptance for these transgressions depends on the extent to which these women obey the other norms: you can absolutely go out with hairy armpits if you are conventionally attractive. Just as female politicians have already broken one rule of 'femininity' by accessing a place of power, and therefore must obey all the others, famous women with normative physiques, as long as they do obey all the others, can skip hair removal. Or, rather, *some* hair removal: armpits with hair, but everywhere else without, or legs with hair as long as it's discreet and there isn't much of it. The bikini line, moustache and chin remain non-negotiable.

On the other hand, the demands for hair removal are so stringent that often the media make out that an armpit with a little, almost invisible, downy fluff, which must have been shaved all of three weeks ago, is a flagrant transgression of the norm. The penalty applied to unshaven (or not sufficiently well shaven) women, which is undesirability, doesn't apply to these actresses, models and singers. They are unquestionably desirable *despite* not shaving, because they have so many 'desirability points' that it doesn't matter if they lose a few.

Long hair, a highly potent symbol of femininity, is another example. The idea that only conventionally attractive women can wear their hair short without being branded as butch is based on precisely the same belief. You can only give up such a potent symbol of femininity to the extent that you are extra desirable in every other aspect. Many women believe they *can't* shave their heads because they're not 'pretty enough'. Wearing their hair long or short, the same as shaving their armpits or not, is only a choice for those who 'can afford it' – that is, for those who won't see their femininity or desirability questioned, because they adhere to the established canons of beauty. For everyone else (that is, the majority), there's no choice: as a minimum, you have to strive for maximum desirability. This means being conventionally attractive, but also being white and upper-class. Women who suffer racism and/or working-class women receive even more negative comments (gross, filthy, disgusting) if they don't shave than do upper-class white women, in whom it's considered a forgivable eccentricity (again, only if they conform in every other way).

One fascinating example of self-exclusion sought for reasons that have nothing to do with shattering the gender binary is the appearance in China of tights that give the effect of having very hairy legs. They popped up in 2013 in response to the many sexual assaults which occurred on public transport, and the idea was that hair on legs would dissuade sexual aggressors, who would be repulsed by hairy women and not assault them. Even though these tights didn't become popular, remaining an oddity, it's interesting to analyse the reasoning that led to their creation: rather than growing your hair and that's that, you add it in certain situations where you think looking 'less feminine' can help you suffer less violence. The obligation for women to shave is so inflexible that, even when (from the most perverse patriarchal perspective possible) having body hair could 'save you' from being raped, this hair must be false so as not to threaten your 'inherent femininity'. In the sense of making oneself 'less desirable', one of the recommended tactics for reacting to a rapist is to belch, fart or vomit, if these are things you can do on cue. In some cases, appearing 'disgusting' can dissuade the attacker. It goes without saying that the causes of sexual assaults are not shaved legs or how 'desirable' the victim might be, but rape culture and the impunity of rapists.

One study published in 2019 in the *Journal of Sexual Medicine* shows that, while men are more satisfied with their affective–sexual relationships when their partner fulfils their expectations about shaving, women are more satisfied when they fulfil their partner's expectations. That is, while one bases their satisfaction on having what they desire, the other bases it on being desired. That isn't innate (desire is learned), or fixed (what is desirable changes over time and according to culture), or banal (it's part of the framework of inequalities that we endure).

As a woman, fulfilling society's expectations in regard to shaving implies submitting to this power dynamic, giving up the position of a subject who desires and accepting the role of an object of desire. It means reinforcing a culture that subjugates our pleasure to that of others, and continuing to teach (others and ourselves) to desire an aesthetic that demands pain, money and time to be maintained, without obtaining anything more than the approval of others (which is no small thing, I know) in exchange.

When considering the possibility of dissent in the expression of gender implied by not shaving themselves, not all women have the same freedom: there are those who exclude themselves from traditional femininity, and, on the other hand, those who need to display a very binarized gender expression in order to suffer less violence.

We might think that lesbians can easily escape the trap: if they don't have affective–sexual relationships with men, they should be beyond noticing the male gaze on their bodies and, therefore, should feel more free not to shave. However, the construction of desire, as much for heterosexual men as for homosexual or bi women, begins from the same base. A desirable woman (for whomever) is a shaven woman. You only have to watch the iconic series *The L Word* to notice it. It isn't the fact of not having male partners that makes some lesbians and queers break the norm of hair removal: if they break it, it's due to conscious positioning against the binary system of gender expression. Having hairy legs takes you immediately out of the 'desirable woman' box (for men, obviously) and, in fact, adds a question mark to the category of 'woman'. This is an advantage for women seeking a visible break from the laws of heterocentric desire, who already want to stand out from the heteronormative at first glance. Obviously, this doesn't spare them the discrimination that comes with being read as a diesel dyke.

Regardless of sexual orientation, showing body hair publicly is a kind of neon billboard saying 'I don't follow the gender norm of hair removal', and any derailment in gender expression breaks the mirage of heterosexuality by default. For that reason, the supposed choice between shaving or not is never innocent. Not doing so places you on the side of the rebels, and possibly as a frigid dyke feminist (no matter which, if any, of these categories you actually occupy). Doing so positions you – in principle, and as long as you don't break any other norm – as the good, submissive heterosexual woman. That is, not shaving doesn't make you more lesbian or more feminist, but it will make people who don't know you categorize you as such almost immediately.

Choosing a non-normative gender expression is to announce publicly that you don't submit to the gender binary. What's more, if you are a woman, you are demonstrating that you don't conceive of yourself as a potential sexual object and explicitly reject being boxed into the established canons in order to be liked. For that reason, it's not enough to have a partner (of a non-binary gender, woman or man – it doesn't matter) who doesn't care whether you shave or not, or have no partner if you don't want one, to feel free not to shave. In addition to a dissident sexual practice or orientation, you have to feel prepared to suffer the discrimination suffered by everyone who doesn't appear to be cis hetero.

Not all women live in the same circumstances, or enjoy the same rights in reality. In theory, everyone has the right to bodily integrity, but we know in practice this isn't always attained. For someone passing as a cisgender woman like me, who doesn't suffer racism, who lives in a quiet neighbourhood in a small city, with freelance work in a theoretically progressive field, with a network of friends and family that is very committed to disrupting gender, it's incredibly easy to have a non-normative gender expression. I've rarely worried about whether I'm at risk of violence (partly because I consciously avoid certain situations), whether I have hairy legs or not.

The gender identity of cisgender women is not questioned. They don't have to *demonstrate* that they are women, because the people who would question it are content with checking for particular genitalia or some documents that declare it: cisgender women have a cunt and a birth certificate as final proof of their supposed *feminine essence*. They can afford to be a woman *even if they don't look like one*, from a general perspective. These ideas are clearly transphobic, but unfortunately very common, and they make it very difficult for trans women, who can't supply the same 'proof' as cis women, to break gender norms in tandem with their gender expression.

Removing body hair is part of the expression of gender that isn't considered performative but, rather, essential: choosing to have it is incompatible with adhering to gender norms. 'Girls shouldn't have body hair', which recognizes a social norm, becomes 'girls don't have body hair', which denies the obvious reality. In the ultimate paradox, the false notion that women don't have body hair even infiltrates the ads for hair removal products, in which models shave hairless legs. The vague concept of body hair is tacitly recognized because of the commercial interest in the need for hair removal products, but the existence of hair that must be eliminated is denied.

If hair removal is obligatory for all who don't want to have their womanhood questioned, it's even more so for those questioned by default for not passing as cis (that is, because they're visibly trans). There are some traits that help us in the immediate, slapdash classification we make of people as man or woman when we see them. Clothes, beard, length of hair, make-up, visible body hair are the first things we use. If they all point to one conclusion, we don't give it much thought. If any of them fail, we look at the breasts or package. If these don't stack up either, we focus on the voice, the size of the hands, the Adam's apple . . . For a trans woman, wearing skirts with shaven legs and not having even a trace of a beard can be the difference between passing unnoticed (and therefore being safer in public) or drawing attention as someone disrupting gender norms and coming under attack from strangers.

Cis women *can afford* to give up shaving because *they don't need it* as a proof of their supposed intrinsic femininity, while, on the other hand, trans women are exposed to constant questioning of their gender and are required to comply fully with the norms of gender expression, to the utmost extreme.

Hair in certain areas is such a powerful marker of gender that the majority of women (trans or cis) who have hair on their chin don't even consider not removing it. Those who decide to leave it are few, and they find themselves constantly facing other people's doubts about their gender. What invests authority in men, who are seen as mature and wise when they sport thick beards, is unacceptable for women. Bearded women have traditionally been circus flesh and material for ridicule, or objects of fetishization. Obviously, the fetishization of female body hair isn't limited to the beard, and in fact is based on the same idea that the bodies of women are only acceptable according to the extent to which they endorse the male gaze. You must shave, except if your male partner doesn't want you to.

The absence of body hair is immediately associated with femininity and, in fact, men who don't have body hair are seen as *effeminate*. In the last few years, there has been a boom in male hair removal, but just as women who don't shave have to fulfil the other demands to preserve their *femininity*, men who shave have to be 'very masculine' in everything else in order to leave people in no doubt as to their heterosexuality. Otherwise, they would become the 'not so manly men', who are gay. When the adjective *metrosexual*, referring to men who take care of their appearance (for example, shaving their backs or chests), became fashionable, the first part of the definition was 'heterosexual man who . . .'. It was taken for granted that taking care of your appearance, using moisturizers and shaving parts of your body were feminine activities directly associated with homosexuality. This belief isn't exclusive to the cis-hetero collective: sissyphobia – that is, discrimination against men who are 'too feminine' in their gender expressions – also exists among gay men.

Even though we often confuse gender expression (how I present myself to the world so my gender identity is understood) and sexual orientation (for whom I feel desire), it's clear that they don't necessarily go hand in hand. The insults *fag* and *dyke* don't usually refer to the orientation of the person insulted (which is impossible to know if they don't declare it), but to their nonnormative gender expression (which can indeed be seen at a glance). The less discriminatory the environments in which we live, the greater the freedom we have to adopt less normative gender expressions. Those women lucky enough to be able to shatter the norms of gender expression without suffering much violence should take advantage of their position to try to make a change in the collective imagination that will allow more and more people to be educated.

The artist Rocío Salazar, a cis woman who at that time was in a heterosexual relationship, began to go out in public with hairy legs. Her partner let her know that he was made uncomfortable not by her hair itself, but by the fact that his friends might see it. This pushed the artist to do some research and she produced a study about why it's so disturbing when women stop removing their hair. Through simple drawings with very direct captions, Salazar exposes the double standard regarding body hair: 'I don't mind you having it, as long as no-one sees it.'

Far from being a personal, exceptional experience, it seems that what bothers men about their partners' hair isn't the hair itself, but that other men might think them 'less of a man' for going out with a woman who is 'less of a woman'. Socially, a woman who doesn't shave and is partnered with a man brings the manhood of her partner, who should control her better and make her conform to gender expectations, into question. Breanne Fahs, a professor of Women & Gender Studies at Arizona State University, proposed that her female students stop shaving for two months and keep a diary of how this affected their lives. The reactions of the students' circles were illuminating: 'Have you asked your partner's permission yet?' 'You say he doesn't care that you're hairy but surely it must bother him. He just doesn't want to make you feel bad.' 'Are you turning into a lesbian?' 'Gross!' 'You'll never get a boyfriend.'

The desirability of a hairy woman is less actual (that in practice their partners might find them less attractive) than social. Not shaving during the winter, when the body isn't on show, is normal among women and has no impact on their sexual life, especially when in long-term relationships. However, as soon as the body is on show, the hair must disappear, or they risk being considered not 'womanly enough' or not 'good women'.

It's fascinating that the hairless body, the fruit of a social mechanism such as hair removal, is considered a sign of *innate* femininity. It would be logical for body hair, which separates the girl from the woman, to be considered intrinsically feminine (and even sexy). However, we've reached the point where it's the contrary.

And I find that deeply worrying.

4

Because I Want To, Sure.
But Why Do I Want To?

The majority of women who shave truly believe they are doing so because they want to. Therefore, perhaps a more interesting question would be not why they shave, but why they *want to*. The primary reason – 'I feel more attractive/better/prettier' – is clear: you feel prettier hairless because all the models of beauty you've had since you were born were hairless, in the same way that you feel prettier when you're thinner, when you wear your hair long, when you put on make-up, when you wear conventionally feminine clothes, etc. A cliché of films and TV series is 'the fake ugly girl' – that is, a girl who is presented as undesirable and who, on various grounds, is 'transformed' into a 'real woman'.

This transformation usually involves going from tying their hair back to letting their hair down, from trousers to a dress, from buttoned-up to buttons undone, from glasses to contact lenses, from a bare face to made-up. There is also usually a hair-removal scene, which, in the case of legs, usually consists of shaving invisible hair, and can also include shaping eyebrows. All the tools of traditional femininity are deployed to 'uncover' the beauty the character has always had. It's curious how this process of artificializing the body is presented as a way of getting to the *essence* when, in fact, layers of supposed masculinity are being removed yet what remains isn't an intrinsically female body, but a body that must indeed be covered with layers of supposed femininity. The process is so fascinating that it has passed from fiction to reality TV, and there are various programmes that consist of astonishing the audience with 'how pretty this girl who at first seemed so ugly really is'. Even programmes like *Skin Decision*[1] which show the before and after of

[1] *Skin Decision* is a Netflix reality series first released in 2020, in which two participants in each episode undergo plastic surgery to alter an aspect of their appearance that they dislike.

cosmetic surgery procedures claim that surgery will release 'your true self'.

The more feminine the person wants to be, the further this 'true self' moves from the 'natural version'. The level of artifice required of men and women in order to be regarded as 'presentable' enough to go out is totally asymmetrical: men have to be clean, hair combed and in clean clothes, so that with a shower and a change of clothes, they're done. If they want to, they can shave, but having a beard is also acceptable. Women, however, haven't even got started with a shower and change of clothes. What's more, there's a difference of a few hours of treatments, drying and brushing between washing your head with long hair (as it's preferable for women to have) and washing your head with short hair (as it's preferable for men to have), not to mention the absolute ban on women having white hair, which makes men 'more interesting' but means unending tinting sessions for women. Hair removal, extending every day to more parts of the body, comes under the 'required minimum' for women, which incurs a significant investment of time and money. The efforts can have tangible results, like hair removal, or imaginary ones, as in the case of many supposedly

43

toning, anti-wrinkle, anti-cellulite, anti-ageing creams. In the end, in this fight against the body, what counts when being a proper woman isn't only the results: if there aren't any, at least you've made an effort to achieve them.

The social and cultural mechanisms that lead us to consider certain representations of femininity as more attractive are difficult to ignore. However hard I try, I can't help it: having identified as a woman for most of my life, I too feel prettier when I'm hairless. But again, perhaps we're focusing on the wrong thing? So what if I don't feel especially pretty when I haven't shaved?

The idea that women must always be 'pretty' is about permanent sexual availability: as objects of desire, they have to be ready if at any moment some man looks at them. In the experiment we discussed in the previous chapter, in which Breanne Fahs suggested her students stop shaving for ten weeks, the comments made by many of the girls' families were: 'You'll never find a boyfriend like this', or 'Your partner won't find you attractive anymore.' We don't like ourselves with hair 'where it shouldn't be', it's true. But the underlying fear and constant threat is that *men* won't like us.

The obligation of trying to please is added like a deadweight to the rest of the daily demands on women and piles on additional pressure – especially on women with less normative bodies – that they should spare themselves from. The fiction of the woman who fits perfectly and effortlessly into the canons of beauty is a harmful one, not only because it's false (the models and actresses we see as gorgeous when 'just out of bed' and dressed in 'any old thing' have entire teams behind them, dedicated to fabricating this falsely natural and spontaneous image), but because it denies the quantity of time, effort and money that women spend (and men are spared) to get close to this ideal. It naturalizes a process that could not be more artificial, with the constant threat of not being liked if they skip it.

Magazines like *Cuore*[2] that 'unmask' famous women with photographs of unkempt hair, cellulite, comfortable clothing and other crimes against good taste could be a weapon against the narrative of a supposedly 'natural' perfect image – they could air the idea that not even the most

---

[2] *Cuore* is a weekly Spanish tabloid magazine, first published in 2006.

45

stereotypically pretty model is always perfect. But they do the exact opposite: they become a kind of witch hunt in which women are ridiculed for not being permanently prepared for the scrutiny of the femininity police. They present it as totally unacceptable to relax, even minimally, the obsession with presenting an immaculate appearance, even for activities completely unrelated to their work as models and actresses, such as walking the dog, being at the beach or going shopping. What could be 'Don't worry, no one can live up to these demands 24 hours a day' becomes instead 'Watch out, you'll be ridiculed if you don't follow the rules in all circumstances.' *Cuore* describes itself as 'the only magazine that will increase your self-esteem', but it's another cog in the machinery that makes women's self-esteem depend to a large extent on social approval of their image.

Trends like body positivity – which advocates that all bodies are beautiful – and body neutrality – which advocates that the body, beautiful or not, allows us to live and this is sufficient reason to accept it and love it – can help immensely in freeing ourselves from the chains of a femininity that demands time, money and pain from us. On one hand, recognizing that the norms of beauty that seem impossible to break are in reality cultural constructs that change over time and space can help us to accept our bodies. The ruling canons of beauty are so strict that questioning them and trying to see the beauty of other kinds of bodies can in itself be a very freeing first step. However, we can't deny that what we consider 'a really beautiful body' is burned into our brains, and for women, among other things, this means a hairless body. So, if I don't like myself with hair on my legs (or armpits, or bikini line), before giving in to the norm, perhaps I can ask myself: will the world end if I'm not pretty? The answer in the majority of cases is 'No'.

As long as you're not part of a vulnerable group (where, if you don't meet certain aesthetic norms, you could lose your job or suffer an increased risk of violence in public), the consequences go no further than glances and comments. One of the most freeing aspects of breaking a gender norm is realizing that in practice it doesn't affect our lives as much as we had imagined. In the end, the most paralysing threat is about the acceptance of others. This threat – which is connected to the fear injected into women since birth of not being respected, desired or loved if they don't bend to the demands of the patriarchy – makes them do really outrageous things, if we look closely at them. One way of deactivating the threat is by confirming that there are indeed people who will respect us, desire us or love us *despite* our not fulfilling the norms. But, beyond this indisputable fact, there's a question we must ask ourselves. Why do I want to please everyone all the time? Do the benefits of social approval make up for what it costs me? And, beyond whether I'm likeable or not, have I thought about who I like and why? Do I want the approval of someone who finds me disgusting when I've just got up in the morning?

Moving from perceiving oneself as an object of desire that obeys gender norms uncritically, to believing oneself above all to be a subject who assesses her options before bending to the rules, is a much more profound process than simply giving up shaving. But without this process, it's difficult to stop shaving, because the punishment/reward system incentivizes us to do it.

Believing we'll get reproachful looks and negative comments on our body hair – that is, we'll get many comments we won't like – can cause anguish. To navigate the anguish of 'not pleasing', we can relax in the assumption that not shaving doesn't necessarily have to be a definitive, total decision. We can stop shaving the areas we feel laziest about, or that are the most painful to rid of hair, or that give rise to the fewest complexes. This is different for everyone: there are women who cannot bear to imagine themselves with hairy legs, but can perfectly tolerate not doing their armpits, and vice versa.

Knowing that at any given moment, for whatever reason, we can shave if we want can take away the enormity of the decision. We can decide not to shave in general, but do so for special occasions on which we want to feel particularly comfortable with our appearance. This shifts the *obligation* to please, and changes it to the *will* to please: today, when I want to feel attractive or my appearance is especially important to me for some reason, I shave. Obviously, being able to feel comfortable and sexy without shaving would be ideal, but it's easier said than done. Focusing on how often it happens that you *want* to please can be an interesting exercise.

Another reason women shave is because it seems 'more hygienic' to be shaven than not. Even though men's bodies aren't innately cleaner than

49

those of women, nor is their hair known to have implemented some sort of self-cleaning system, this norm doesn't apply to them. So, while a woman with hair on her legs – or especially her armpits – is considered dirty and disgusting, this doesn't happen to men.

There is no existing study that claims that having body hair is associated with more odour or dirtiness than if we remove it, and, on the contrary, there are a number which demonstrate that removing hair from certain areas, especially shaving it, can provoke health problems. A study published in the *American Journal of Obstetrics and Gynaecology* in 2014 shows that almost 60 per cent of women who shave their pubis have experienced problems relating to hair removal, especially abrasions and ingrown hairs, and around 4 per cent of this number have had to seek medical attention as a consequence.

Another study, published in the *Infectious Diseases in Obstetrics and Gynaecology* journal in 2017, found a correlation between hair removal and vulvar intraepithelial neoplasia, which involves pre-cancerous cells that grow on the skin of the vulva. The sample size was very small, featuring only 47 women with cancer and a control group of 247 healthy women, so this isn't a conclusive study, but it's worth bearing in mind.

It's also been shown that the habitual practice of shaving an area before operating, theoretically to prevent infections, not only doesn't work, but actually increases the risk. Removing hair from an area with other methods, like wax or hair removal creams, isn't as harmful as shaving, but doesn't reduce the risk of infection compared to leaving the hair as it is. Hair can 'trap' bacteria, but this is precisely so they don't reach the skin, where they proliferate more easily. There are just as many bacteria in an area without hair as in an area with, but the difference is that, in the latter, it's much more difficult for them to reach the skin, and we are therefore better protected.

On the other hand, the small cuts produced on the skin when we shave our pubic hair (and very often we can't even see them) increase the possibility of sexually transmitted infections (STIs) as well as boosting abrasions, with more injuries and a higher risk if both (or more) people involved are shaved.

Removing hair doesn't improve hygiene, and in fact can be prejudicial for health. Just as we do with many of our habits, we evaluate the risks and benefits and don't always decide in favour of what will most benefit our physical health, because there are many other factors at play. However, saying you shave because it's more hygienic is like saying you smoke because you breathe easier: it goes against all scientific evidence.

Many women who understand all these facts say they continue to shave because it's a practice they've totally internalized, but they will try not to perpetuate this chain and will leave their daughters free to decide whether they want to do it or not. This is like men who say they would have no problem with their sons wearing skirts, but never wear them themselves. Without powerful, familiar models, it's difficult for a child to see the possibility of breaking an obvious gender norm that everyone follows to the letter. Telling a boy, 'You're free to wear a skirt', or a young girl, 'You're free not to shave', is cruel if they're not offered support in facing the ostracism they will experience. If I don't feel ready to face the social punishment that follows not shaving, if I'm not capable of overcoming notions of self-worth based on physique and external approval, if I don't take the risk of challenging the gender norm, how can I expect my daughter, who doesn't have the experience and weapons of an adult woman, to do so? What kind of freedom am I helping her to conquer if I don't dare take it for myself? Will I truly respect her decision and avoid making comments on her body hair if in the end she doesn't shave?

Women shave because they want to, indeed. But what they want isn't shaving in itself, but to avoid paying the price demanded of them if they don't do it. A curious freedom, at the very least.

5

A Hairy Road to the Future

I'd decided not to shave anymore.

Every new expedition in public with my legs on show, every lunch at my in-laws in shorts, every work meeting not worrying about my underarms made the decision easier. The bubble around me gives me an unrealistic image of society, I know. Few comments, and every one respectful along the lines of 'Oh, I see you don't shave anymore', followed by congenial chats. The people who don't like it simply don't say anything. It's easy for me.

I'd decided not to shave and I stuck to it, but there was one thing that flustered me a little: I couldn't wear dresses. The image of skirts, an undisputed symbol of femininity, with hairy legs, an undisputed symbol of masculinity, was paralysing my brain. I didn't feel good about it at all. So I basically spent two summers in trousers.

Discourse that questions norms, which takes us out of docile obedience to what impedes our self-fulfilment, is necessary. But clearly it's not enough to change an archetype that has been spoon-fed to us since birth, to wrench from ourselves a self-loathing absorbed from all around over a lifetime. However clear it was to me, and even while transitioning into a non-binary gender identity, I continued seeing myself as ugly, or at least inadequate, if I tried to dress 'as a woman', with all that visible hair. The same impulse pushing me to buy ever-longer swimwear that covered my bikini line full of hair (but free of cuts and spots too) stopped me wearing the dresses that had been with me every summer for over ten years.

It's naïve to think that, simply because we process certain ideas intellectually, this will automatically change our most deeply rooted emotions: Beliefs and prejudices are so difficult to change because, even though they're shown to be irrational time and again, they cling to a feeling that is deep and much more difficult to sway.

But if, despite understanding that hair removal is a gender norm with no meaning at all (like all gender norms, it must be said), we continue to see ourselves as horrible when we don't do it, how do we end this vicious circle? If, even when we decide to emerge from the toxic dynamic of wanting to please at all costs, we keep not pleasing ourselves? One possible answer is 'out of conviction', which wouldn't be the most powerful reason for the majority of people.

There is good news, however. The obligation of hair removal goes two ways: on one hand, we have the models presented to us by hegemonic discourse, which, in short, tell us that a woman should only have hair on her head, her eyelashes and her eyebrows. But on the other hand – and to a great extent thanks to the feminist, body positivity and body neutrality movements – every day there is more flexibility in having hair in certain areas, in certain circumstances.

This can be seen when we look at the data separated by age: one study by the company Mintel from 2018 shows that young women are more tolerant of body hair than older women: 25 per cent of women between 18 and 34 years of age consider it acceptable (which is not the same as desirable) to show armpit hair, as opposed to only 5 per cent of women of 55 years of age. In the same twenty years that shaving almost the whole pubis has become commonplace among young women, the number of women who don't think it a sin to have hairy armpits has quintupled.

Many women who can afford it – because it's not cheap – have succumbed to the benefits of laser hair removal: with a number of sessions, you can forget hair removal forever. Some women gift it to their adolescent daughters, so they can avoid the torture of wax and razor. It surprises me that it doesn't even cross their minds that they might regret it. What if one day they find themselves missing having hair and they can't grow it anymore? It's strange that the questions asked when someone announces they're getting a tattoo don't happen in the case of permanent hair removal: everyone finds it perfectly understandable that someone would want to get rid of body hair forever.

Social norms seem inflexible to us while we suffer from them (or benefit from them, depending on which side we find ourselves), but they are actually continuously changing. If, instead of clinging on to the restrictive norms of our generation, we dare to transgress, we are opening a way for younger women to stop considering their hair disgusting. I'm not sure the time has come for me to feel sexy with hairy legs, but showing them may contribute to others in the future feeling themselves to be so. And, all in all, for the times when I want to feel sexy, I find ways to achieve it *despite* the hair. Hopefully, someday it will also be *thanks to* the hair.

A friend who has also given up shaving mentioned not long ago that the act of giving it up and *nothing happening* has liberated her on many other levels. If I've broken this norm, to which it seemed impossible not to adhere, and not been struck down by divine lightning, what others can I break?

Saying that shaving or not has no importance, that it's a decision women take freely, is denying reality. Right now, it's still extremely important – symbolically, for those lucky enough to have their rights respected, but above all in practice for those who suffer violence so extreme that not shaving could literally cost them their lives. Saying 'I shave because I want to' makes the mechanisms of social control invisible, because it doesn't take into account the reasons for this 'preference' and underestimates the consequences of choosing an alternative, but it also subtracts power from the possibility of not doing so. By making out that it's a banal decision we are robbing ourselves of the possibility of agency in bending some suffocating gender norms.

Psychologists say (as does a study by Philips that wants to sell us, in this case, an ultra-modern and extremely expensive epilator) that hair removal improves women's self-esteem. In reality, hair removal on the one hand reinforces the idea of beauty that we have internalized, and on the other prevents verbal (or even physical) violence to us. It's true that it's easier to have high self-esteem when you're not the target of scorn and insults. However, the solution should be respect, rather than hair removal. I can shave and save myself problems, but I can't control what others do. Therefore, many women 'decide' to shave even though, if they could, they would 'decide' that there were no consequences from not doing so. Collectively disobeying the rule would avoid the pointing and staring, because the exception would cease to be so.

The majority of times in my life that I've shaved, I've done it 'for me'. To feel prettier;

because I didn't want to worry whether I was getting disagreeable looks; because I was more comfortable in the invisibility offered by following the norm. In short, to please others (or even myself). And now that I've decided not to shave anymore, I'm also doing it for me. Because I don't want to waste any more time on it, because it hurts me, because I'd never allowed myself just to go to the beach without even thinking whether I had to shave or not, and the truth is I've gotten a taste for it.

I've bought myself a new dress. It's very plain, made of cool fabric, soft against the soft hair of my body. It shows only my calves, I feel good in it. I put it on and go for a walk, determined.